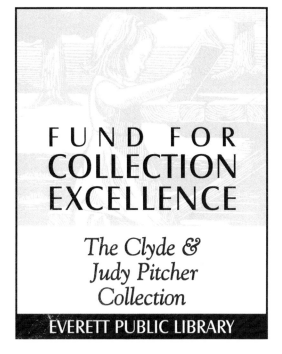

CONTINENTS

ASIA

by Bethany Onsgard

Content Consultant
Martha Chaiklin, PhD
University of Pittsburgh

CORE

Published by ABDO Publishing Company, PO Box 398166, Minneapolis, MN 55439. Copyright © 2014 by Abdo Consulting Group, Inc. International copyrights reserved in all countries. No part of this book may be reproduced in any form without written permission from the publisher. The Core Library™ is a trademark and logo of ABDO Publishing Company.

Printed in the United States of America,
North Mankato, Minnesota
042013
092013
♻ THIS BOOK CONTAINS AT LEAST 10% RECYCLED MATERIALS.

Editor: Blythe Hurley
Series Designer: Becky Daum

Library of Congress Control Number: 2013931968

Cataloging-in-Publication Data
Onsgard, Bethany.
 Asia / Bethany Onsgard.
   p. cm. -- (Continents)
ISBN 978-1-61783-930-6 (lib. bdg.)
ISBN 978-1-61783-995-5 (pbk.)
1. Asia--Juvenile literature.   I. Title.
950--dc23

                                        2013931968

Photo Credits: Shutterstock Images, cover, 1, 8, 11, 20, 25, 27, 33, 41, 42 (top), 43 (bottom); Red Line Editorial, Inc., 4, 24, 32; Sean Pavone Photo/Shutterstock Images, 6; Galyna Andrushko/Shutterstock Images, 12; Yury Taranik/Shutterstock Images, 14; Daniel Prudek/Shutterstock Images, 17; Boris Diakovsky/Shutterstock Images, 22; Pete Niesen/Shutterstock Images, 28; Pavel Svoboda/Shutterstock Images, 31; Sharon Kennedy/Shutterstock Images, 36; Jeerawut Rityakul/Shutterstock Images, 39; Sergey Uryadnikov/Shutterstock Images, 42 (middle); Pichugin Dmitry/Shutterstock Images, 42 (bottom); Arvind Balaraman/Shutterstock Images, 43 (top); Yuri Yavnik/Shutterstock Images, 43 (middle), 45

CONTENTS

QUICK FACTS ABOUT ASIA

- **Highest point:** Mount Everest, Nepal, 29,035 feet (8,850 m). This is also the highest point in the world.

- **Area:** 17,226,200 square miles (44,615,653 sq km)

- **Distance north to south:** 5,465 miles (8,795 km)

- **Distance east to west:** 5,515 miles (8,876 km)

- **Key industries:** Oil, fishing, manufacturing and technology, metals, textiles, agriculture

- **Population:** 4.2 billion

- **Five biggest cities:** Shanghai, China; Mumbai, India; Karachi, Pakistan; Delhi, India; Istanbul, Turkey

- **Three most common languages:** Mandarin, Hindi, Russian

CHAPTER ONE

WELCOME TO ASIA!

Asia is the world's largest continent. It stretches all the way from the Arctic Circle in the north to south of the equator. Asia occupies huge portions of the Eastern and Northern Hemispheres.

Population

More people live in Asia than on any other continent. Four billion people call it home. Some of the world's

Mount Fuji is one of Japan's most well-known landmarks and serves as a symbol of this Asian nation.

Shoppers and merchants selling their goods fill a busy street market in Bali, Indonesia.

most populated cities are scattered across this huge continent. These include Shanghai in China, Istanbul in Turkey, Karachi in Pakistan, and Mumbai in India.

Yet Asia also has some of the world's most unpopulated areas. Subzero temperatures in the northern region of Siberia and unpredictable weather in the Gobi Desert keep the populations in those places quite small.

Asia is so huge that it is often broken down into six different regions. These are Central Asia, Northern Asia, Eastern Asia, Southeast Asia, Southern Asia, and the Middle East.

The Great Wall of China

On the biggest continent on Earth, you'll also find the longest structure. This is the Great Wall of China. It is about 13,171 miles (21,197 km) long. The Great Wall is actually many different walls built by different emperors over hundreds of years. The first section was built from 256 to 206 BCE to keep the Chinese people safe from outside invaders. Chinese builders did all this work without modern machinery.

Angkor Wat

Angkor Wat in Cambodia is one of Asia's most popular tourist destinations. It is also the largest religious monument in the world. King Suryavarman II built this enormous temple during the early 1100s. It was originally dedicated to the Hindu god Vishnu. Later it became a religious center for Buddhists. This temple is a source of great pride for Cambodians. It is also one of the United Nations' World Heritage Sites.

Culture

Asia is the most culturally diverse continent in the world. Asian people speak over a hundred different languages. They are a part of many different religious and ethnic groups. Islam and Judaism are widespread religions in the Middle East. But in other areas, Daoism and Buddhism are more common.

Landmarks

Asia is home to many of the world's most famous landmarks and natural wonders. Tourists flock to the Great Wall of China and the Taj Mahal in India. Asia is also home to modern attractions like the Petronas

The giant Buddhas of Angkor Wat stand watch over an ancient temple, which is now also a popular tourist attraction.

Twin Towers in Kuala Lumpur, Malaysia. These are dazzling, 88-story twin skyscrapers.

Borders

People do not always agree about where Asia stops and Europe begins. In some areas, there are no clearly drawn boundaries. Russia lies mostly in Asia. But it becomes a part of Europe on the western side of the Ural Mountains. Geographers also consider Turkey to be a part of both Europe and Asia.

CHAPTER TWO

ASIAN LANDSCAPES

Asia's six regions all have very different climates. Some have miles of tropical ocean coastline. Others are mostly cold, snowy tundra.

Central Asia

The Gobi Desert is the largest desert in Asia. It takes up a huge part of Central Asia. The word *gobi* means "waterless place" in Mongolian. There are only two

The Gobi Desert's lack of water and wide variety of temperatures make it an inhospitable place for human life.

This lake is a part of the Altai Mountain Range, where Russia, China, Mongolia, and Kazakhstan meet.

to eight inches (5 to 20 cm) of precipitation here each year. Water is a valuable resource for people who live in this region.

Many people think deserts are always warm. But the Gobi Desert has a wild variety of temperatures. In the winter, temperatures can reach a freezing -40 degrees Fahrenheit (-40°C). These temperatures, along with the dry soil, make it difficult for crops to grow. Most people live in the more hospitable lands near coastal areas.

Northern Asia

Northern Asia is home to even fewer people than the central region. This is because of its cold, snowy weather. Siberia, in the northern part of Russia, takes up most of Northern Asia. In the areas closest to the Arctic Ocean, the climate is so cold that summer only lasts for one month. Temperatures of -40 to -60 degrees Fahrenheit (-40°C to -51°C) are normal for Siberia in the winter. Because of the cold weather and frozen soil in the north, most Northern Asians live in the southern part of this region.

Eastern Asia

Eastern Asia has over 31,800 miles (51,177 km) of Pacific Ocean coastland. Eastern Asia includes China, Mongolia, North Korea, South Korea, and Japan. It also includes over 3,000 islands in the Pacific Ocean. These areas have very warm climates in the summer. But they often suffer from monsoon rains and typhoons. Typhoons are what scientists call hurricanes that occur in Asia.

Many Eastern Asians live along ocean coastlines. Coastal farmlands are perfect places to grow rice, an abundant crop in the area. Fish is an important food for people in areas near the coast. Away from the ocean, the landscape is very mountainous and rocky. This makes it hard for people to grow food.

Southeast Asia

Just like Eastern Asia, Southeast Asia has both mainland countries and island nations. Most of these countries lie on or near the equator. This means the climate stays warm and tropical almost all the time. The average temperature is 80 degrees Fahrenheit (27°C). In the wet season, which is Southeast Asia's winter, heavy rains sweep in from the Pacific Ocean. This provides water for crops.

Southeast Asians tend to live in the wet regions near the ocean or near one of the area's many rivers. Rivers such as the Irrawaddy, the Chao Phraya, the Mekong, and the Red River all provide enough water to grow crops.

Buddhist prayer flags decorate one of the base camps where climbers prepare to ascend Mount Everest.

Southern Asia

Southern Asia is surrounded by the Arabian Sea, the Bay of Bengal, and the Indian Ocean. Southern Asia has rainy summers and dry, warm winters. This makes it a popular place for people to live. In fact, in 2011 almost one out of every four people in the world lived in Southern Asia.

This region also has many mountains. This includes the Himalayan Mountain Range. The Himalayas are home to Mount Everest. This is the

The Sherpa People

Climbing Mount Everest is not easy. Most of the people who attempt the climb hire a guide to help them. The Sherpa people, who live in the villages around the base of Mount Everest, are known around the world for their mountain-climbing skills. Sherpas guide climbers up to the summit. They also rescue stranded climbers who need help getting back to base safely. Approximately 4,000 people have made it to the top of Mount Everest.

tallest mountain in the world. Mount Everest stands 29,035 feet (8,850 m) above sea level.

The Middle East

The Middle East is one of the driest, flattest places on Earth. The soil is usually not good for farming because of the desert conditions. But people have figured out how to live with the little water they have. The Tigris and Euphrates Rivers run through this region. These provide water to the surrounding countries. The people of the Middle East have developed sophisticated irrigation systems. Irrigation systems bring water to dry areas in order to grow crops.

Sven Hedin, a well-known Swedish explorer during the 1900s, was one of the first Westerners to document a journey across Asia. The passage below from his journals tells of traveling across the Gobi Desert during the winter of 1927–1928:

> The storm lasted the whole night, and on the morning of the 14th of November it roared and howled and raged still worse than on the day before. Out in the open not a soul was to be seen. All kept under cover, even the weather-hardened Mongols. The deserted ground looked as if a broom had swept over it. Light-coloured comet-tails of dust and sand wound their way along over the ground with the speed of the wind. Whenever one walked among them, one had a feeling of insecurity . . . it appeared as if the earth was moving and as if one must sink down in its restless billows.
>
> Source: Sven Hedin. Across the Gobi Desert. London: George Routledge & Sons, 1931. Print. 251.

Back It Up

In this passage, Sven Hedin uses descriptive language to make a point about the safety of crossing the Gobi Desert. What point is Hedin making? Write down two or three pieces of evidence he uses to make his point.

CHAPTER THREE

ASIAN PLANT AND ANIMAL LIFE

Some of the world's most unusual animals live only in Asia. This includes Bactrian camels, Komodo dragons, Siberian tigers, and giant pandas. All of these animals are endangered species. This means that only small populations of these animals are left in the wild.

Bactrian camels roam through the rocky deserts of Central Asia. They have long, shaggy hair that

Giant Pandas are one of the world's most beloved animals, but loss of habitat has dangerously decreased their population in the wild.

Bactrian camels have evolved to thrive in harsh desert environments.

protects them from the cold. They shed this hair when the hot summer months arrive. Bactrian camels have two humps on their backs that store enough fat to sustain them during long trips across the desert.

Komodo dragons have long, muscular tails and scaly skin. They can grow to be ten feet (3 m) long and weigh 330 pounds (150 kg). They are the largest lizards on Earth. Komodo dragons are dangerous animals with sharp claws and teeth and poisonous saliva. They live only on the islands of Southeast Asia.

Siberian tigers once roamed Russia's forests. Today they are very rare. They are the largest of all the wild cats in the world. Siberian tigers can grow up to 660 pounds (299 kg). Their striped coats keep them camouflaged. No two tigers have the same stripes.

One of Asia's most recognizable animals is the giant panda. This black and white bear can grow to up to 300 pounds (136 kg). Giant pandas are also known

Rice

Rice is a type of grain, like wheat or corn. It is one of the most widely eaten foods in the world, especially in Asia. Scientists and historians disagree about where people first began to farm rice. But it has been an important crop in China, Japan, India, and many other parts of Asia for thousands of years. Rice does well in areas with high rainfall. It can grow successfully on land that is difficult to farm, including steep hills and mountains.

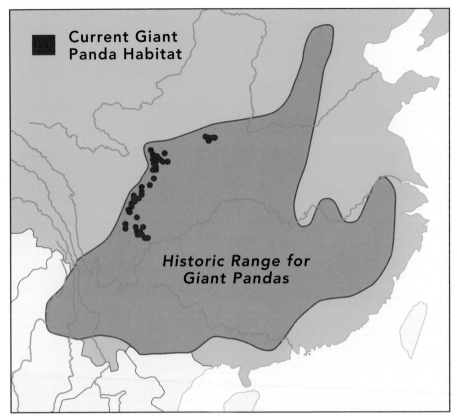

Current Giant Panda Habitat

Historic Range for Giant Pandas

Giant Panda Habitat Reduction

Giant pandas once roamed a habitat that included much of southern and eastern China, as well as neighboring Burma and Vietnam. Now the pandas' territory has been reduced to a handful of tiny areas in China's Tibetan Plateau Mountains. How do you think this loss of habitat has affected panda populations? What might the Chinese people and government be able to do to help pandas?

for their eating habits. Almost 99 percent of the

food they eat is bamboo. They spend almost

12 hours a day eating. It takes almost 28 pounds

(13 kg) of bamboo a day to feed a full-grown panda.

The Japanese people treasure the temporary beauty of spring's cherry blossoms, such as these blooming near Himeji Castle.

Plants

Asia also has many interesting plants, including the giant panda's main food source, bamboo. Bamboo is actually a grass. It is one of the fastest-growing plants in the world. It can grow up to 24 inches (61 cm) a day. People in Southeast and Southern Asia eat bamboo shoots. People also use bamboo as a building material.

In Japan people celebrate the beautiful cherry blossoms that appear in spring. These pink flowers grow on *sakura* trees. People bring blankets to parks to have picnics while enjoying the beauty of the flowers. There's no time to wait, since the blossoms fall to the ground about a week after they bloom.

Tea grows throughout Southern, Southeast, and Eastern Asia. It does best in warm, wet climates. Ginseng, which is grown primarily in China and the Korean Peninsula, is exported throughout the rest of the world.

The Corpse Flower

Rafflesia arnoldii is known for its unpleasant odor. This is why people also call it the corpse flower. It also produces the world's largest flower. Corpse flower blossoms grow to be about 39 inches (1 m) across. That's larger than a beach ball. These plants grow only in the rainforests of Southeast Asia. They have no leaves, stems, or roots. They also do not have chlorophyll. They take all their water and nutrients from other plants, upon which they grow. The corpse flower is an endangered species.

This rare *Rafflesia arnoldii* blossom blooms in Malaysia on the Southeast Asian island of Borneo.

EXPLORE ONLINE

Chapter Three focuses on the animals that live in Asia. It also talks about endangered animals. The Web site below also focuses on endangered species. As you know, every source is different. How is the information in this Web site different from the information in this chapter? What information is the same? How do the two sources present the information differently? What can you learn from this Web site?

Asian Endangered Species
www.mycorelibrary.com/asia

CHAPTER FOUR

THE PEOPLE AND CULTURES OF ASIA

Before cars and airplanes, Asia's many mountains and deserts made it hard to travel between regions. The desire to trade eventually caused people to begin to travel outside their home regions. Asia was a source for spices, silk, and other goods. European and African countries wanted to trade for these items.

A Mongolian woman wears traditional clothing during the Naadam National Games in Ulan Bator, Mongolia.

The Silk Road

Silk was an important commodity in ancient Asia. There was high demand for it in the West. Traders traveled the Silk Road using camel caravans. They brought silk, jade, and gold from Asia to Europe. Many travelers and historians have called the Silk Road the crossroads of the world. People and goods from many cultures once crossed paths on this road.

Trade and Religion

Trade routes sprang up between Europe, Africa, and Asia. These trade routes also increased the spread of religion. In fact, people often call Asia the birthplace of religion. This is because it's where many of the world's most important religions began. Judaism, Hinduism, Buddhism, Islam, and Christianity all began in Asian regions. These religions have since spread across the globe.

Religious Celebrations

Religion is still very important to many Asians. Many of the continent's holidays and celebrations are religious in nature. Hindus celebrate *Diwali*, "the

An ancient tower still stands in Kyrgyzstan on the route of the famous Silk Road.

festival of lights," in the fall. They light candles and fireworks on Diwali. During *Loi Krathong*, the festival of floating bowls in Thailand, Buddhists float bowls of flowers down rivers and canals. They believe this sends away all bad luck for the coming year.

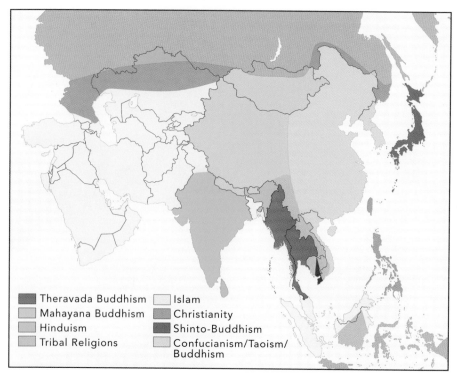

Religion in Asia

This map shows the areas where some of Asia's major religions are practiced. Are you surprised by how many different religions have spread through this vast continent? Do you think a similar map of North America would have as many different religions? Why or why not?

Entertainment and Recreation

Many Asians both watch and play football, which Americans call soccer. They also enjoy table tennis and badminton. Baseball is very popular in Japan. Some Asians also play cricket, a game similar to baseball.

This young woman from Hong Kong is dressed in costume as a character from a manga comic book.

In Japan, people of all ages read *manga*, or Japanese comic books. This art form now has fans all over the world. Bollywood, India's version of Hollywood, is home to a booming movie industry.

Diversity

There is no one Asian culture. People on this continent speak over a hundred different languages. They have many regional food preferences. People in coastal areas eat a great deal of fish and other seafood. Vegetarian dishes with rich flavors such as turmeric and curry are common in the Middle East and India. Asian people are as varied as the land they live on.

The Asian Games

Much like the Olympics, the Asian Games is a multisport event held every four years. Any Asian country can participate. These games feature many of the same sports as the Olympics. But they also include traditional local games, including *sepaktrakraw*. Sepaktrakraw is a Southeast Asian sport sometimes called kick volleyball. Players are forbidden to use their hands and arms in this sport.

Suketu Mehta is an Indian-born journalist who grew up watching Bollywood films. In this excerpt from a *National Geographic* magazine article, he writes about his experience sharing Bollywood films with American friends:

> *Most Westerners—if they've even seen a Bollywood film at all—find them far too unsophisticated and melodramatic. Most are three-hour-long extravaganzas in which the stars frequently break into elaborate song and dance numbers. The plots are far-fetched, built on coincidences and unrealistic expectations. The actors change costumes . . . and locations . . . multiple times within a single song. But the audience doesn't mind. Like fans of Hollywood films of the 1930s and '40s, Bollywood fans want to enter a magical realm where the impossible is possible, where true love conquers all, where history is defeated by sentiment.*

Source: Suketu Mehta. "Welcome to Bollywood."
National Geographic *February 2005: 52-69. Print. 53.*

What's the Big Idea?

Take a close look at Suketu Mehta's words. What is Mehta saying about Bollywood culture and how it differs from entertainment in the United States? What evidence does he use to support his point? Come up with a few sentences showing how Mehta uses details to support his main point.

CHAPTER FIVE

ASIA TODAY

Asia is just as diverse today as it was thousands of years ago. New technology has helped create new industries. But many regions still rely on agriculture to earn money.

Growth

It's estimated that Asia's population will reach 4.7 billion by the year 2050. With so many new people being born in Asia every year, it is getting harder

The Hewadori Market in Okinawa, Japan, offers foods many Westerners might not be familiar with.

Bullet Trains

Many Asians use buses, bikes, and trains to get around every day. One modern method of transportation that was first used in Japan is the high-speed bullet train. These trains can travel up to 185 miles per hour (298 km/h). In December 2012, China opened a 1,200-mile (1,931 km) bullet train route, the longest ever completed.

to feed them all. Many children in India today are malnourished. And 59 percent of Asians live on less than two dollars per day. Poverty and hunger are problems for many Asian countries. People and governments throughout the world are exploring new ways to grow enough healthy food for everyone.

Economy

Eastern Asia is home to many successful technology companies. Asian companies such as Toshiba, Sony, and Samsung make many of the phones, televisions, and electronics used in the United States. Hyundai, Honda, and Mitsubishi make cars for customers around the globe. China is a leading exporter of steel,

Machines build cars on an assembly line in an automobile manufacturing plant in Samut Prakan, Thailand.

iron ore, copper, and tin. These exports make Eastern Asia a world industrial power.

Natural Resources and Agriculture

In Eastern Asia, many people make their living along the coasts by fishing. Many people throughout Southern and Southeast Asia still make their living as farmers. Rice is by far the most important crop throughout Asia. It is common in many Asian countries to see rice laid out to dry along roads at harvest time. The economy of the Middle East is mainly based on the petroleum industry. Oil is an abundant natural resource in that region. There is high demand for it in other countries.

Rug Making in the Middle East

Rug making has been a traditional part of several Middle Eastern cultures for thousands of years. These floor coverings were important in harsh climates to control dust and hold heat inside homes. Most people now use machines to produce carpets and rugs. But rugs made by hand in countries such as Afghanistan and Pakistan are still popular around the world.

Looking Ahead

Asia has problems to face in the future. These include protecting its wildlife and improving the lives of its less-fortunate people. But Asia is also home to wonders from both the modern world and the past. Asia has much to offer both those who call it home and those who come to visit its many lands.

Farmers in Vietnam often grow rice in terraced mountainside farms.

FURTHER EVIDENCE

Chapter Five shares information about the fishing industry in Asia. What was one of the chapter's main points? What are some pieces of evidence that the chapter uses to support that point? Check out the Web site at the link below. Does the information on the Web site support the main point in this chapter? Write a few sentences using new information from the Web site as evidence to support the main point this chapter makes about fishing in Asia.

The Japanese Fishing Industry

www.mycorelibrary.com/asia

The Taj Mahal

The Taj Mahal in India is one of the most recognizable places in Asia. Emperor Shah Jahan built this large, marble building in 1632.

The Taj Mahal

Komodo National Park

The Indonesian government created this national park to protect Komodo dragons and other wildlife. The park is on three islands, including the island of Komodo.

A Komodo dragon devours its prey.

Grand Palace

The Grand Palace in Bangkok, Thailand, is one of that country's most famous landmarks. It was built in 1782 and was the home of Thailand's kings for over 150 years.

The Grand Palace in Bangkok, Thailand

The Tian Tian Buddha statue of Hong Kong

Tian Tian Buddha

People often call the Tian Tian Buddha statue in Hong Kong "the big Buddha." This giant golden statue stands 112 feet (34 m) tall.

The Great Wall of China

The Great Wall of China

Most of the popular sections of the Great Wall of China are only a short trip from Beijing, China. Visitors are allowed to hike sections of the wall.

The Dead Sea

The Dead Sea

The Dead Sea, which borders Jordan and Israel, is the lowest point on Earth. Swimming in this nutrient-rich sea is said to alleviate the pain caused by diseases such as arthritis.

STOP AND THINK

Why Do I Care?

Traders used the Silk Road and other ancient Asian trade routes thousands of years ago. But international trade with Asia is still important in our world today. How does trade with Asia affect your life today? Are there traditions that might not exist if Asian, European, and African countries had not begun to trade along the trade routes? Use your imagination!

Take a Stand

This book discusses the fact that Russia and Turkey are a part of both Asia and Europe. Do you think countries should be able to be part of two different continents? Or should there be clearer borders drawn to avoid confusion? Do borders and continents really matter in the daily lives of people there? Write a short essay explaining your opinion. Make sure to give reasons for your opinion, and share facts and details that support your reasons.

You Are There

This book discusses how people in many Asian countries eat and sell the things that grow and live near them. Imagine you could only cook or make a living off the things you find outside your door. How would this change your daily life? What kind of jobs would your parents be able to do to earn a living?

Say What?

Learning about other countries and cultures can mean learning a lot of new vocabulary. Find five words in this book that you don't know. Use a dictionary to find out what they mean. Then write the meanings in your own words, and use each word in a new sentence.

GLOSSARY

camouflage
coloration or patterns that help an animal blend with its surroundings

chlorophyll
a green pigment present in all green plants that is responsible for the absorption of light to provide energy

commodity
a raw material or agricultural product that can be bought and sold, such as copper or coffee

hemisphere
half of the globe, divided into Northern and Southern Hemispheres by the equator and Eastern and Western Hemispheres by the meridians

malnourished
suffering from improper nutrition or not having enough to eat

precipitation
rain, snow, sleet, or hail that falls to the ground

summit
the highest point of a hill or mountain

tundra
a vast, flat, treeless Arctic environment found in Europe, Asia, and North America in which the layer of soil beneath the topsoil is permanently frozen

typhoon
a violent storm or hurricane in the western Pacific area of the China seas

LEARN MORE

Books

Barnes, Trevor. *Hinduism and Other Eastern Religions*. New York: Kingfisher, 2005.

Ceceri, Kathy. *The Silk Road: Explore the World's Most Famous Trade Route*. White River Junction, VT: Nomad Press, 2011.

Clayton, Sally Pomme. *Tales Told in Tents: Stories from Central Asia*. London: Frances Lincoln Limited, 2004.

Web Links

To learn more about Asia, visit ABDO Publishing Company online at **www.abdopublishing.com**. Web sites about Asia are featured on our Book Links page. These links are routinely monitored and updated to provide the most current information available. Visit **www.mycorelibrary.com** for free additional tools for teachers and students.

INDEX

ABOUT THE AUTHOR

Bethany Onsgard is a voracious reader, a cookbook collector, and a craft enthusiast. She attended the University of Minnesota and now works in book publishing in the Twin Cities. She lives in Minneapolis, Minnesota.